WHAT THE BUTTERFLY SAID

(Metaphysical And Philosophical Poems)

By

Thomas P. Lind

WHAT THE BUTTERFLY SAID

ISBN 978-0-9800989-5-2

LIND PUBLISHING, 210 Foxwood Dr.
Brandon, Florida 33510-4013
Ph. 813 681 2551
mailto:tom.lind@live.com

Fellow Humans, "be a lamp unto yourselves, be a refuge unto yourselves, betake yourselves to no external refuge, seek not for refuge from no one but yourselves. Be a fully enlightened, a self-enlightened one."

"Only I and the Buddha's of The Universe

Alone can understand these things

The truth beyond demonstration

The truth beyond the realm if terms."

The Buddha.

WHAT THE BUTTERFLY SAID

Have a no limitation's belief; because it is by our beliefs, we create our faith; and boycott our potential. Through the quiet assurance of our inner resolve and the confidence of our inner knowing, we can manifest the good, the true and the beautiful in our lives; positively, with the limitlessness of imagination and an open mind and balanced heart the abundance of the Universe is at our disposal,

Seek not for salvation by external means,
Seek not to know thy self by external effort,
Seek not to know the truth by the discursive
mind.
For the truth lies in our undifferentiated
Absoluteness at the center of our being.
*This is the essence of reality,
Where we are fulfilled.

Advertence

A person may be dedicated to his beliefs and opinions, and sincere about their intent, but that does not mean that they are true or factual. Because he is identified deeply with them, he holds them to be true and would die in defense of them. My deference to these people is one of the understandings; but the irony is, they do not know; they are living a life of self-deception. They are so convinced their beliefs, and options as it was instilled in them are the absolute truth, they condemn all those who do not believe as they do. We should not stand in judgment or condemnation of one and other, for in all reality; we know not what we do.

WHAT THE BUTTERFLY SAID

The Self is the Self-
Identifying power of life;
It has the power to move and
Whole worlds of butterflies emerge;
It utters a word, and they fly!
Thomas P. Lind

If you think, the Universe is complex,
Just look at yourself under a microscope.

Hallucination is contagious,
The whole world suffers from it.

We need not be perfect

We need not be Saints

Nor we need be a Demon

We need to be our nature

Which is to be Human!
Thomas P. Lind

The majesty of a waterfall
And the delicate beauty of a butterfly
Have no distinction in an Artists' eye!
Thomas P. Lind

As a Butterfly was waving
The infinite sky, its' beautiful
Multicolored wings radiant against the
Brilliance of the sun; it delicately
Alighted on a red rose whispering,
Saying, not by the randomness of whim,
We are privileged to express beauty
Differently, grasp intuitively,
That, to "truly" know God is to be God.
Thomas P. Lind

INTRODUCTION

We should honestly; constantly search for truth, not with those who think they have it—those who think they already have it, will never find it.

Why do I write? Because I want to bring to our attention nine basic concepts, which determines how we live and view our existence. They are Ignorance, Greed and Hatred; Wisdom, Contentment and Love; The Absolute, Infinity and Eternity. The first three have had devastating effects on us individually as well as socially; the other six are beneficial. Ignorance, Greed and Hatred do not only affect us materially, but also mentally, emotionally and spiritually; they have been the predominant, controlling, destructive attitude through the ages. Consider all the wars, conquests and colonization's, and the ravaging, devastation and annihilation of people and their cultures, all the crimes, defrauding, looting, murders, torture and rapes. I consider these destructive mental attitudes. I advocate their eradication from our minds, our hearts and our societies. On the other hand, Wisdom, Contentment and love are the redeeming spiritual factors; the wings of hope lifting us above the sinking sand, the quagmire of the swamps; propelling us to the peak of the mountain to reveal the magnificence of our humanity. The Absolute, the infinite and the eternal are the most abstract, sublime, encompassing concepts of the human mind. Because we can envision them, we get a glimpse of immortality.

The spirit is immortal, and in itself has no shape, but it has the power of individuation and self-consciousness. On the other hand, the physical body is not immortal. However, physical immortality is a biological possibility achievable when we have altered the DNA's genetic code and made the cell immortal. Making the cell immortal will entail regulating the division, the regeneration and the maturation of the cell, making the telomeres indestructible, making the cell impervious to toxic chemicals and environmental changes. We have to learn, how by mistaken impulses cells destroy themselves, and how to reverse unhealthy programing.

Physical life began at the cellular level. The cell is very intelligent and adaptive. It is the evolution of the cell, from unicellular to the multicellular with the specialization and the division of functions, which created all the different species of animals, birds, butterflies and humanoids on the planet. It is my firm belief that whether we achieve physical immortality by science or not, we are headed for immortality by natures means. Because the life force which sustains and regenerates the cells is indestructible. In a way we are already intentionally helping and accelerating our evolution by the application of the various sciences, we have extended our life span and lifestyle. Our intellection and physiques are improving daily; and by the accumulation and rapid communication of knowledge, our world is expanding exponentially for a better future.

We have come a long way from Adam and Eve, or whatever geneses, we attribute to our origin; and we have traced our ancestry to one lineage D.N.A. Through long ages of struggle, wonder and wandering; we developed an open mind; we became more intimate, and less fearful of our surroundings, the environment and the universe. At what age we became intelligent, no one knows; it seems it was a gradual process, which is still unfolding; neither does anyone know, when we become self-conscious as a species, nor as an individual. However, those two attributes are what sets us apart from all life forms on the planet, and perhaps in the universe.

This self-consciousness is innate, is a reflection of our self-identifying power, through the attribute to create and sustain thought and give expression to think by vocal sounds; it utters the first thought by word, which is "I am." This confirms our identity as an individual in the physical world. From birth to death this sense if identity never leaves us, except if the brain becomes disease and is unable to manifest it; the power identity tells us who we are, and that we are no other than what we are. That we are different from other life forms, perhaps through the cosmos. The faculties to express thoughts by vocal sounds and visual imagery, is what gives us the unlimited power of creative imagination. Hence, forth from the first thought and words "I am," we've created Heavens and Hells, Universes without end; from the cave to penthouses and city skyscrapers, from flint stone spear heads to the atom bomb—from one thought to the innumerable constructive as well destructive and confusing.

Mysteries can be amusing or horrifying, but they are not virtues; they may stir our emotions, but they are not pointing to some truth, which we cannot intellectually grasp. Those who make virtues of them are indulging in their ignorance. They do not only indulge in their ignorance, but also they perpetrate this ignorance to the credulous and the gullible. Moreover, ignorance is the precursor of greed and hatred. They are delusional, denying their senses and the reasoning of their rational minds, living an illusion. What we consider mysteries is only assumptions we make about events and occurrences, which we do not understand, because we do not have all the facts. The things we do now, which we take for grand, and are commonplace events in our lives like talking and conveying our ideas to others thousands of miles apart, or transporting our bodies through the air, from one place to another, thousands of miles around the world, would have been magical and mysterious to our ancestors five hundred years back. Therefore, the things, which appear mysterious to us now, will be commonplace to those who proceed us five hundred years hence.

Besides that, nothing is permanent, as recently; scientists are coming up with the String Theory, saying that the ultimate reality is wavy strings of energy. So actually, our reality, at all levels, is what we say it is. Ponder this, how many times, the postulates we considered scientific factual reality, by which, we thought the Universe was governed, and we governed ourselves, has changed over time.

All the above should prove, that the Self-identifying power (our sense-of-self), the Knowing principle and the Life principle are one—the Knower, the Knowing and the Known are inseparable, and insuperable. In addition, it is the self-identifying power, which gives certainty and permanency to our existence. The greatest miracle is that our lives are endowed with this knowing, moving self-identifying power, which we call self-consciousness—it's this self-identifying power, which tells us with certainty, when we wake up in the morning, that we are the same person who went to sleep the night before—not our self-concept.

However, it is our self-concept, which smothers our sense-of-self, which is yelling, I AM that I AM—without any descriptions or qualifications. Furthermore, it's our self-concept, which says: I am good; I am evil, beautiful, ugly, happy, unhappy, contented, discontented; alternatively, I am rich; I am sick; I am poor; I am a Doctor, an Architect, a Lawyer; a destroyer, defrauder, murderer, thief. Moreover, whatever we say we are, as surely as the sun will rise every morning, we become.

He who discovers infinite intelligence, will live in the absoluteness of his Being—his eternal self—that core

root of energy that transforms, and blooms into the magnificence of a Human Being.
Thomas P. Lind,
Brandon, Florida,
December, 2015

PRELUDED

Certitude is a gut feeling, that we comprehend, beyond the realm of terms.

QUANTUM BUTTERFLY

What the Butterfly said: I am a multicolor illusion of mist, as the rainbow made, flying allusive space and time. As I flutter here and there, it may seem I made a "Quantum Jump" without flying through the air, but sometimes I wave my wings, sometimes I perch. Those who observe me claim they behold me, saying they really see me flying through the air.

Some claim I am not there, until they see me flying through the air; when they collapse my waving wings to a particle. Some say that whatever flies near me become entangled with me forever; wherever, however, far apart we may go, we influence each other. Oddly enough, Michel Angelo and Leonard, although inspired, could not find the space to contain me in there canvases and rocks. Galileo was under house arrest because he said he saw me flying far away orbiting the sun; and there came along Aquinas with his syllogisms saying, he solved the mystery; it was the creative mind and hands of God who make me. He said, "To one who has faith, no explanation is necessary. To one without faith, no explanation is possible." In addition, here is how he further explains it: "God should not be called an individual substance, since the principle of individuation is matter."

The Butterfly said, whatever said, about me, does not explain why I am a Butterfly—an illusory butterfly; nether reality nor the truth can be described, they are only known intuitively.

FLYING BUTTERFLIES

We arrantly peruse the Butterfly,
As it flies, the sky's fluting here and there,
Taking it from our senses and thoughts.

Why do we give the Butterfly freedom?
To fly, restraining ourselves to touch,
Seeing, to hearing, to smelling, tasting?

Why we create the illusion of space
And time, restricting to where we can go?
All we need to know we are free to fly!

Limit not our imagination;
To know freedom, the mind must be detached,
Abiding, but do not cling to a cloud!

Vivid imagine as the Butterflies.
Fly the boundless skies along with the clouds;
Let not a thought arise to hinder thee.

Stars may seem randomly placed in the sky;
Neither they nor ants climbing up the hill;
For all by an impulse of thought, are made!

An Artist's Hands

Looking upon the ocean

Admiring its depth fearing its fury

I lift my eyes up to the skies

I wonder whom how

I lower my lids begging

Forgiveness my ignorance why

Looking at a flower I see

An artist's hands intentness

The advertency of a leaf

Ornamentations of the earth

The Butterfly

I feel eternity as I inhale exhale

I climb I swim I walk

Exhausted exhilarated I sprawl

AWAKE FROM YOUR SLEEP

Awake from your sleep!
To another dimension where
You can see the ties which
Hold you earthbound; from
Which you can swirl as a Butterfly
Through the forests unharmed.

Unchained, fly the oceans as
The seagulls beyond all illusory
Horizons. Disentangle from
The web of imagination, untie
Yourselves from the ropes of
The emotions; Unwrap from the
Wrappings of your thoughts.

Fear not enter the dimensionless
Dimensions, for this is your
Eternal home. Rest in the
Tranquility of the Absolute;
Sleep serenely as the Angles do.
Repose in the strength of your soul!

A GOLD COIN

Kindness is sacred; it is among
The Divine gifts. I saw a bird
Flying through the skies, hurriedly,
To place a worm at the reach of
Its awaiting offspring. What joy!

If I could give you a Gold Coin,
It would be the fragrances of
The winds after flirting with
The Pines. If I can leave you with a
Melody in your heart and joy.
It would be music from beyond;
It would be wings as butterflies!

If I brought to you a gift from the
Skies, as nightly in my dreams
I fly, it would be to tell you,
In my sleep I am told, all would
Be well on earth, if we acted
As if, we were in Heavens. Now!

BOUNDLESSLY EXCEEDING

When we have arrived
At an infinite, intimate knowing,
Without the prop of a thought,
Beyond the impulse of a sensation,
The shades of emotions, we need
Not to strive for immortality.
We are Immortal!

We are from timeless time at
Beginning without form, without end.
Our soul's always sores the skies
Surpassing where butterflies flies.
It permeates the trillion of trillion's
Stars, boundlessly exceeding
The contrivances of imagination.
Then we know who we really are!

AFTER THE RAINS THE SUN SHINES

We must stop castigating
Ourselves by our erroneous
Belief; the chastening by our
Deviant thoughts has proven
Unfruitful. There is a Prototype
Within us perfect and eternal.

It brings forth the child and
Persists throughout the ages.
It's the Perfect You with a
Flawless mind, which unfortunately,
Deviates from its originality.

Entrapped by the fleeting impressions
Of an evanescent world. We can
Only return to our center, our
Absolute Self, our Absolute Identity
By eschewing this illusory world
Of our making.

Stand aside and ask,
yourselves, to whom are these senses,
Feeling and thoughts occurring?

WHAT THE BUTTERFLY SAID

You'll see them as alien stormy
Clouds; and the Self as the sun, will
Always be shining, after the rains!

BUTTERFLIES ADORNS THE SKIES.

Cast thy bread upon the waters,
And know it returns double fold
On the crest of every wave.
Look afar upon a star, and know
Its light shines in every heart.

Cast your gaze on the clouds, and
Know its rains replenish the earth,
And flowers will bloom again;
Butterflies will adorn the skies.

Compassion is the spiritual love
A soul has for another, and every act
Of Human Kindness is a gift,
Of unconditional love!

Butterflies and humming birds
Adornments of the skies
Alights on the beauty of roses
To reveal eternity by a flower
Infinity as they fly!

THE EYES OF BUTTERFLIES

Wings of mystery,
Canceling furies of the winds.
Souls fearing blown to shreds,
Speak hope in varied tongues;
Sailing the deep blue skies.

So many wings smashed,
Clouds blocking the way.
Hail the Mary's of the world!
Mothers of spring,
The gates of Heaven swing

Persistent waving wings
Until the eyes of men
Angels have seen!
Oh, sing to the world
Of Joy to bring!

HIDDEN TREASURE

Where the winds do not stir,
Nor the crackle of sand heard,
The leaves do not move;

There in solitude reveling
The Absolute; there in the silent
Symphony of eternity,

There in the infinite is where
The Butterflies abide. There, behind
All our thoughts, they hide.

TO INFINITY

From the middle
Of nowhere,
A thought rises.
Mountain peaks
Covered with snow.

All around below
Rivers freely flow,
Gloriously Flowers blossom,
Birds eternally fly.

Through the Heavens surely
Butterflies
Aviate their wings
Lions proudly roar!

To infinity they go!

FOREVER

Painters paint with a rush, a poet, with words.

Skies dripping

Clouds whispering domes

Aroma of distancing waterfalls

Twisting river foam disappearing

Shadows of walls mountain shades

Winds teaching birds to fly holding hands

Hand gliding over precipitant waves

Butterflies unperturbed endure

Skies compressing molecules of love

Vines of life clinging blossoming flowers

Forever!

PARA SIEMPRE

Los pintores pintan con pincel, el poeta, con palabras.

Pringues de cielos

Nubes que susurran cúpulas

Aroma de cascadas distancias

Enrosca desaparición espuma del río

Paredes de sombras crepúsculos de montaña

Vientos que enseñan aves a volar agarro de manos

Mano que se desliza sobre ondas precipitadas

Las mariposas impasibles duran

Cielos que comprimen moléculas de amor

Ramas de engancho de vida florecen las flores

¡Para siempre!

SECTION II

BEING GENUINELY HUMAN

BEING GENUINELY HUMAN

Every judgment we make is a predicate of our ignorance; we cannot make the Human Spirit subservient to our whims. We have been trying to rationalize our spirituality for generations to no end. In addition, we adore our illogical conclusions on an altar of logic of wrong premises. Our philosophies are redundant reflections of the intellect of a squirrel revolving in a cage of its making. Those who theologize and politicize are gambling with our freedom, and therefore, are losers at the end. The Spiritual in a human cannot be incarcerated, enslaved, or confined by dogmas or creeds, for it has no form, color or shape, no beginning, no end! To be genuinely human is to realize we exist in two worlds simultaneously, the implicit and the explicit, in the formless world of the spirit and the material of the body. However, we are not two separate entities as traditional philosophy and theology tell us. We are as two faces of the same coin. It is this dichotomy, the classification of everything to two opposing parts, bodied and souls, heaven and hell, us and the universe prevalent in our systems of thought, which is the cause of all our frustrations, hatred, anger, rage, and existential anxiety. We have to hold hands across the world, transcend cultures and ethnicity, and proclaim our rights of citizenship of planet earth.

I have always envisioned that there will be an Empire of the World, but not an empire of authoritarian dictatorship; one of collaborations and collective effort, that would respect life and the rights of the individual to share in the resources of the planet and eliminate hunger—prejudice, bigotry and discrimination. We have to replace dogmas with truth, ignorance with wisdom, greed with altruism, hatred with unconditional love.

It's not by chance goodness.
Prevails; our Holiness derives
From the Devine light that
Ignites the sparkle of love
In the heart of every man,
Woman and child. It ignites
The firmaments lightning up
The skies, and lights the light
For every ant climbing a hill.
It makes every grain of sand
A stepping stone to Heaven.
Every act of generosity and

Gratitude is Devine expression
Inherent in our Human Potential!
Goodness is not a reward,
It's a Devine award of merit
For being Genuinely Human!
Awake! And be thy Self!

DO UNTO OURSELVES

By our beliefs, we create our faith,
But, it's by our faith we hold onto
Our beliefs, right or wrong.

 If we, then instead, would have
 Unlimited beliefs, we would have
 An indestructible unlimited faith.

It should dawn upon us, we
Are infinite, pure beings ,
Transcending all eternity,
Absolute in its own essence.

 Every act of Human Kindness would
Then be its own reward, as what we do
Unto others, we do unto ourselves.

ANGLE FREE

No one is prejudices free,
Not even science, nor how
Pure our intentions may be.

Our perceptions are tinted
From the angle we see;
Our interactions are biased by
The experiences we've had.

Every thought we think we have
Is a thought someone else has had;
We are partial without intending to be.

To really see what we see comes
Only to a perception angle free;
A mind freed from the mind itself!

CONTINGENT LIFE

Something necessitates our existence,
As we necessitate it, otherwise neither it,
Nor we would exist, nor the Universe.

Existence exists because it exists,
As its own cause, nothing exists
Outside of it that can
Explicitly or implicitly, explain it.

No matter how intense our desires to change
It, it remains as it is for all eternity.
It knows we depend on it, and won't
Let us down; life is contingent on it.
Nonexistence is a non sequitur!

THE KINGDOM OF GOD

If the Kingdom of God is within
Us, and God resides in His Kingdom,
As stated in the sacred text we believe,
Why do we go outside of ourselves
To find God? And why we don't
Recognize that Kingdom in each and
Everyone of us? All we should need
To do is go within in silence and
Humility, and behold the Kingdom
Of God; and dwell in His everlasting
Presence, in peace, contentment and
Gratitude. And respect every Human
As abiding in and sharing the same
Kingdom. Even if it was not, this
Would solve many human problems!
All the treasures of king Solomon
Are of no avail to any of us!
We may pilgrimage the for corners
Of the earth, kneel in magnificent
Man made crystal Cathedrals,
Swim ten laps across the river Jordan
To find God, if we don't have
Him within, we wouldn't find Him!

IT COULD BE

It could very well be
God only responds to our feeling
And emotions in prayer; He
Doesn't care for the loud harrying
Hymns we blusterously display.

The exhibits of blatant deception,
Nor the socialized intellectualizations;
The flouting of ethnic disparaging.
Just the feelings of empathy
And compassion count.

MIGHTY PAINTER HE IS

Mightier than the brush of Leonardo
Is the hands of the master painter;
Sculptures surpassing
Michelangelo's statue of David,
For he has painted nuances of color
Sculptured the shape of the Universe.

He has exulted
The mystical smile of Mona Liza
Which conceals the secret every woman has,
The masculine power of David
Which supports the entire world.

Behold the rays of the rising sum
Sense the delicate light of the moon
The majesty of a waterfall
The soothing songs of running brooks
The graceful flight of a bird.
All electrifies!

The magnetizing, beauty of a woman!
Firmly, prideful and care His chisel
Moved exposing ever subtle hidden form
His brush harmony of colors never seen
All this in its wonderful splendor
are pictures of the physical.

The spiritual is more exquisitely magnificent
But it's hidden from us to unfold.
He knows we've taken all given for granted.
All he is given us is free. Also the
Spiritual, only by desired of the soul, unfurls!

SELF IDENTITY

By what inferential inference
You validate your existence,
The sensations of your senses?
Surely, not by what others say.

Because you have eyes,
Doesn't mean you see;
Because you have ears,
Doesn't mean you hear;
Because you have a mind,
Doesn't mean you know;
Because you have life,
Does not mean you are living!

To see, to hear, to know, and
To live you must let go;
All prejudices and biases
Blocking your flow of
Senses, and your mind,
From knowing whom you are.
Really by unblocking your
"Self-identifying-power"
To say "I am", because I am,
You will know!

PICTURES OF THE MIND.

Do you require a marrow to know
Who you are? If you do,
Know what you see is a reflection
Of yourself-concept; it's only a picture
Of what you think you are.

To know who you really are,
Don't think, just be, and you'll
Discover yourself-identifying power,
Steadfast beyond the processes of thought.
Tranquil, serine unperturbed.

It is by thought everything began.
Beyond the world of thought reality is,
Has always been, and will always be.
The whole world is pictures
Of the mind;
All the pictures of the mind
Are illusory, transitory!

MIND IS THE BUILDER

The mind is the architect who
Builds that which it perceives.
It builds mansions from
The blueprints of imagination
And the substance of thought.

They dangle like flowers in a
Hanging garden in space and time.
Even so, it is only in the present
We perceive
Infinity and eternity, the
Embrace of the Universe, and beyond,
Instantly, in the wink of an eye.

THE SELF, THE MIND, THE CORE.

When we ask, "Who am I?"
If you find by whom the
Question is asked, you'll find
The "I," Then you'll find, that
Neither the question nor the
Answer satisfies. For neither
The "whom" nor the "I" can be
Described, as what you are, is
Only an experience of "That,"
Of which nothing greater can be
Thought off, perceived nor
Conceived. Some call "It" the
Core, the Soul, the Self, the Mind,
Or a Deity by many names.
But a name is just a name!

I SEE A FLOWER

The moment I open my eyes,
I see a flower,
A flower swaying to and fro
Caressed by the invisible hands
Of the winds.

Its fragrance mingling
With the air.
Atoms the atmosphere inhales.

Brilliance by a beam of light pierced
Colors and shapes formed
And heavenly symphonies heard
As sounds, undulate the silence.

I see a flower
And millions and millions more
Are borne!

THE GARDEN OF EDEN

Eureka! Eureka!
 I just had an epiphany,
As I arose from sleep.

I had a vision, that everyone
Was thinking the sane thoughts;
They were all thinking of Love.

 Thinking Compassion, Honesty
 And of Sharing, and Giving
And the whole earth lit,
Vibrating in harmony of song.

 It had turned to Paradise!

Then it really hit me hard,
If it weren't for the billions
Of nonsensical, conflicting thoughts,
We think daily, the earth is
Indeed, a Garden of Eden!

A BIT OF HEAVEN

I got a divine gift I want t to share;
I awoke in the morning in a state
Of euphoria, a blissful state
Pervading the entire body,
The mind, the soul. I neither want
To go back to sleep nor open my eye.
When I was released, my eyes
Opened to the world, I realized,
I had experienced a bit of Heaven!

To be given the gift of perceptual sensing and understanding existence in its essential undifferentiated absoluteness are a gift beyond all the treasures in the world. However, it is a burden and a responsibility, not to be taken lightly; one is driven to at least try to share a glimpse of it with the world—a demanding task requiring, finding embellishing words, to express the most abstruse and abstract concepts. Nevertheless, it leaves a satisfaction in the soul beyond all joy.

THE ABSOLUTE I AM

Indubitably the mystery of
The Universe is unsolvable,
Its greatest miracle however,
Is the manifestation of the Human
Brain with which to behold itself;
And therefore, the Universe as it
Knows itself, and as we know it,
Is a fabrication and a projection
Of the Human brain. The essence
Of the brain is the mind from which
Arises an absolute sense of identity.

Unfortunately, however, among
The many attributes in the mind
Are the random uncontrollable
Production of conflicting thoughts,
Which causes all the dissentions in
The Universe. There is a redeeming
Factor, built in, in which only the
Pure, absolute sense of Identity
Prevails, that is the power to tranquilize
The body and silence the mind,
In the darkness of the night,
The brightness of the day

The absolute "I am" endures.
Paradoxically,
Without shape or form.

No matter how identified we are with the glitter and pleasures of the world, or with negativity and destruction, our sense of Self persists undisturbed through our entire life, even to our last breath. Our hope is that it is immortally preserved. This is the unshakable belief of our religions, the inspiration of our positivistic philosophies.

However, nothing can be asserted or negated about our original Perfect Self, otherwise it would not be perfect. It cannot be known by the intellect only felt by the heart, and it only comes into existence in the act of perceiving. The perceiver, the perceiving and the perceived are one.

Despite all our technological advancements and achievements, we are drowning in a whirlpool of ignorance, ignorance of our Real Nature. The life jackets and the prompts we are holding on to are hindrances to swimming freely upstream to the safe banks on the other side of the river. We dare not to think out of the box, to think the unthinkable, which is beyond all categories of thought; we are afraid we would fall into an abysmal emptiness. However, that indeed, is from where our Self-identifying power emerges.

This is as much as is permitted us to know. All that we think we know is only what we think we know. All our disciplines are only organized system of assumed concrete or abstract thought; the philosophical, the religious, the scientific, and socio-political-economic. They are as ephemeral as a puff of wind, a passing cloud. Moreover, of these, we make structural scuffling, to build our assumed world.

It would behoove us to know that the brain with its many miraculous attributes is an organ as the heart. The function of the heart is to pump blood, but the heart does not discriminate whether the blood is healthy or contaminated. The same with the brain, the main function of the brain is to produce thoughts,   but the brain does not discriminate whether the thoughts are constructive or destructive. This comes from a deeper knowing, that intuitively knows the difference of right from wrong. (Some call it "Conscience," or a sense of right conduct. This is akin to that native intelligence, called, "Common sense." These are terms; we do not hear too often, anymore.)

However, the conclusion is that morality is ingrained deeply in our psyche, because it is necessary to our survival. To kill or to brutalize each other to death, is contra productive. Nevertheless, don't forget that if you are trying to find the Psyche it's at the center of that abysmal emptiness beyond all categories of thought— which is a primary, higher order of existence observed in

the transcendent experience of unbounded consciousness;
the boundless space of a Freed Mind.

ILLUSORY HINDRANCES

Enlightenment is not from the outside
Obtained; the enlightened man needs not
To go outside himself to be enlightened,
Because he is from all eternity enlighten.

Intentionally putting our attention at
The center of our awareness, and effortless
Keeping it there, is to be in atonement
With the core of our being and the entire
Universes, which are, in essence, one.

This is where we erase the attachments
And all the aversions to the glamour,
And suffering, of an illusory world,
Which are, in essence, of our making.

Section III

OUR SPIRITUALITY

A society that denies our spirituality dies,
Suffocating in empirical materialism.
Thomas P. Lind

MATERIALISTIC RELIGION

The unceasing ness of our search for the truth does not abate by our assuming.

Because we are spiritual beings, we seek for our roots in religious expression, but the practice of religion, possibly through the world, is confusing the intent of its purpose, it has become a social enterprise indoctrinating an ethic and a moral, which serves its own purpose.

Most religions today are an intellectualization of our discursive mind formulated into dogmas and creeds, far removed from our spirituality. I call this materialistic religion, because they are based on confabulations, the recall by symbols and images, of social and political events of the past, which are not relevant to our social and political needs now. Historically, religion has not been unifying to the individual, or to the world.

It is true; we have a need for religious expression, because at the core, we are spiritual beings, therefore, our religious practices should be an effort directed to perceiving and experiencing our spirituality in its unmodified, undifferentiated absoluteness. This is achievable when we separate ourselves from all the mental and emotional structures hindering us from experiencing our spirituality at the core of our being.

Roberto Assagioli, Italian Psychiatrist, February 1888-August 1974, pioneer in Humanistic, and transpersonal Psychology, said, "We are controlled and dominated by everything with which the self becomes identified; we can control and dominate everything from which we dis-identify ourselves."

The Human Problem is not one; it is as varied as humans are. I think it is more one of the orientations. As we are born a blank slate, with a few genetic pre-dispositions, but epi-genealogy tells us we are free to create our destiny. We are from childhood told; we are controlled by our genies, but that is not entirely true. We are directed outward, to learn to navigate an impinging, hostile, complex environment. (We are told it is a dog eat dog world, and we become self-fulfilling prophesies.) From, our parents we learn, and from our educational system to do so. This is all very well, because we need certain skills to survive. Nevertheless, it left us with a pervading discontent all our lives, because we are dis-associated from our spirituality, no way along the lines we are told, we are spiritual—that our spirituality demands expression through our religiosity. Religion without spirituality is as our bodies without a soul.

WHAT WE THINK

We are controlled by every passing wind;
Every dark cloud casts a shadow from which
We crouch to hide. We are controlled by
The things with which we are identified.

Our senses and thoughts form the illusion;
We call our world to which we are bound.
We are condemned to live by the stronghold
Of our senses and thoughts, good or bad.

When we are neither attached to them,
Nor abiding with them, we enjoy our
Transcendental freedom. Freedom of the
Mind, from the mind, is ultimate Freedom.

For only what we "Think," is
What we know. Nothing more!
Our beliefs are the thoughts
Of those who thought before us.

WE LIVE BY METAPHOR.

We are a deceptive species
Living a life of "make belief".
.We really don't know who we are,
Where we come from or what
We are supposed to do.
We make belief because we can't
Tell where the illusion begins or ends.
The dream of the night differ
Not in reality, the dream of the day.
To put it succinctly I've said, life is
A drama, we live by metaphor.

I am driven to make these statements, because of the undeniable facts of the turmoil the world is in, not only presently, but historically as well. Self-denial is a part of deception, but the facts prevail. We must ask ourselves, is it human to cause unnecessary pain, suffering and death to people; both in a civilian or war setting? We need not to go any further, because we are witnesses of the disorder; the world has been in and is in today. We do not need any external power, force or authority to guide us, because we have within us the potential to be human. We need to stop the deception and "make belief," and accept responsibility for our existential position in the Universe. Become the genuine Human Beings, we have the potential, and are meant to be.

RELIGIOUS FREEDOM

Religious freedom; Physical,
Emotional and Mental freedom.

This can be accomplished by
Transcending the constrictions
Of our self-concept, the ego
Structure of our empirical mind,
To reach the ultimate freedom.

Transcendental Freedom!
In our true nature; we are
Open Dimensionless Beings!

IN THE IMAGE AND LIKENESS.

The light that shines through
the eyes of every person is only
an individualized reflection of
the presence and power of God.

It's said, we are made in the image
and likeness of God; God cannot
be imaged, as He has no beginning
or end, shape or form. Then, in
essence, we are also image-less,
spiritual beings. It's God's self-existing,
self-identifying power, which informs
the firmaments, the environment,
us and all existing things, all in one
and one in all. All matter is a reflection
of a Divine energy which is at the
basis of all thought forms. At the base
of all thought is a nucleus of energy,
transcending the concepts of
the absolute, the infinite, the eternal,
It's the Presence of God in all things.

The various wavelengths of energy
are transformed into sensations, feeling,
emotions, thoughts and memories.

This we perceive as our existence,
not realizing that its by the power
and grace of God all manifests;
All is sustained. The Human Spirit
Is not subservient to our whims!
The sacred message from all the
Prophets has been, Transform,
Transcend, sublimate, recognize,
Your Divinity!

NOTE:

When I speak of, and use the word God, it is not in the same sense, as any organized religion meaning of the word. It is far removed from any conception, as used in the vernacular, as the God Experience cannot be conveyed by any word or concept; for then, we would be creating a God of our own images. No word or concept can be applied to God for He is absolute in His Essence. Moreover, the Absolute cannot be described; it can only be experienced, and so are the Infinite and the Eternal; without this experiences the Human Experience is not complete.

We claim to be self-aware, self-conscious entities; however, consciousness is not found in our insensate physical bodies after death, the spirit that leaves is self-conscious energy. The objective of this self-conscious energy is to be witness of its existence. Traditional Newtonian physics and scientists don't try to deal with the consciousness phenomenon, as it is intangible, some call it an epiphenomenon. However, there is a new breed of spiritual scientists making deep inroads; for instance, the theories of Quantum Physics read more as metaphysics than those of classic physics.

THAT ARE THOU.

When consciousness becomes
Conscious of itself, it becomes
Aware of its fathomless, crystal
Clear, brilliant, formless, shapeless,
Beginning less and endless nature.

It perceives its Absolute Identity
As stable, unmoved, by all the
Sensations, feelings, emotions,
Thoughts and memories, which
Arise from within itself.

It remains unmoved and unstained
By the input of the five senses which
Are transformed and projected
As the Universe and World.

It realizes this is an illusion which
Dissolves as all thought subsides.
For all from thought are formed;
What we think we are; That we are!

It knows; It's beyond the Absolute,
The Infinite and the Eternal as these
Thoughts also arise from within,
And it exclaims. I am That I am,
Without beginning, without end!

That are Thou, and Thou are That!

We must strive for Political,
Social and Economic freedom;
Religious freedom; Physical,
Emotional and Mental freedom.

This can be accomplished by
Transcending the constrictions
Of our self-concept, the ego
Structure of our empirical mind,
To reach the ultimate freedom.

Transcendental Freedom!
In our true nature; we are
Open Dimensionless Beings!

Because of an erroneous perception,
We conceive ourselves as separate,
Individual beings, floundering in
An incomprehensible evanescent sea
Of sense impressions; but, in essence,
We are one and the same as "That. "
We are one with the same energy field,
From which all springs. And we
Cannot know ourselves by some

Extraneous knowledge, but only by
Our own knowledge of ourselves.
By extinguishing the conditioned
Autonomic negative
Impulses of our subconscious mind,
We sublimate to an image of the Divine!

In our primitive age, we relied on and were attuned to the spiritual world. However, now, for centuries, we have been projecting outward concerned with the impinging complexity of the material world, and material technology advancement's, which in itself are good; however, by ignoring our spirituality; we are living disconnected, frustrating, discontented lives. Let us return to our spirituality. The material is impermanent, transitory, whereas, on the contrary, the spiritual is infinite and eternal—deeply gratifying.

The Self-essence or the Essence-of-self is pure conscious self-awareness, because of this it knows all things, and it's known by all things; in itself, it has no beginning or end, shape or form; as such it doesn't need to know anything; alternatively, to make itself known to anything. Although in itself, it is empty and void, all sensations, feelings, emotions, thoughts and concepts arise from it.

IT'S CALLED A SELF

There is "Something" which to know
It calls itself many things.
It calls itself a "Self", but knows this
Is a formless ephemeral thing.

When it reflects upon the Self, it
Has no shape or form, beginning or end
.It calls itself a "Mind" but nowhere in
Existence can a mind be found;

There are only mental processes
Entangled as in a spider's web.
Reflecting deeper it came to knowing
It is by thought it created itself and
All the imaginary worlds it sees.

Raising a thought in the void
Of eternal consciousness
Focuses a beam of awareness
Manifests the reality beheld!

Through the power of imagination, we can image beyond the limits of the Universe. Through the power of intentionality, we are there instantly and everywhere at the same time. We are an open dimensionless being, a conscious aware energy that sustains existence. A transforming power that knows all things, does all things, and is all things. By the first thought "I am", it assures itself and proclaims, "I am that I am."

WISDOM KNOWS

The eye of Wisdom knows
Everything, whereas the eye
Of Knowledge certain things.

In silence we hear the music
Of the spheres. In solitude we
Are embraced by the Absolute.

Existence is a crest of a wave
Of Eternity. Awareness is the
Duration of the Infinite Now.
Gratitude is thankfulness for all!

WATCHING THE BIRDS FLY

The consciousness of God
Is God's consciousness of Himself.

The conception of God arose out
Of Himself and is implanted in the
Heart every human. It's "That"
Which loves, and, gives the
Spiritual fortitude to overcome
Adversities. It matters not how
Unaware we are of His Presence;
He gives us life and sustains us
To all eternity. He sustains the
Twirling galaxies, the majesty of
Waterfalls; the white sands and
The beauty of the beaches; and
Through us, He beholds, enjoys all!
Watching the birds fly!

THE AWARENESS OF AWARENESS.

Nothing exists until we intentionally
 Put our attention on it,
Then from a vibration of waves of
 Infinite possibilities manifests reality;
 As of, from the focus of our awareness.

 From the shadows in the valleys of
The mind appears beautiful life as
Landscapes, as well as, the phantoms
Of our nightmares. From the center
Of the void blossoms as a garden,
A soul aspiring
Beyond the conjure of all imagination.

The sparkles of creation light the fires
Of love, hiding behind a profusion of
Thoughts and diverting emotions; it
Adds savor, wonder, and mystery to life.

THE ABSOLUTE KNOWING

Absolute Knowing, is
Infinite and eternal knowing,
Which never stops knowing,
By knowing creates itself, all
The subjective and objective
Thing; the mountains, the rivers,
The trees, the flowers, the bees,
You and me.

The Absolute
Knowing beyond the Absolute
Knowing, knowing itself beyond,
Infinity and eternity, is the Absolute.

When it moves out of itself
Onto itself, universes arise.
Its "That," which explodes
Universes from the absolute void!

The import of this poem, which I would like, without
pretention, to impart, is the knowledge of the Absolute,
which is the Absolute knowledge beyond anything we

can think off, conceive or perceive. It's beyond all our sciences, philosophies and religions, yet they cannot be conceived or exist   without it; but, its not of them. It has been passed on from immemorial time, esoterically, exotically, verbally or written, to all who open their minds; to those who gain Freedom of the Mind, from the mind. (To those who see themselves as a reflection in the mirror of the Mind.)   It is the essence of the rose, the soul, hope and love—immortality and Eternity itself!

THE CHOICE IS OURS.

It's the mind that controls the emotions,
Not the emotions that control the mind.
To be in control of our minds and
Emotions are to be in control of our lives.
The mind in itself, as an entity, does not
Exist. All our sensations, feelings,
Emotions, images, thoughts and
Memories are only conditioned
Responses of fleeting neuronal impulses;
Why do we let them determine the
Outcome of our lives? As self-conscious
Beings, we have the power of
Self-awareness and mindfulness with
These, we can guide ourselves and
Dominate the earth. We must extinguish
The mind by the cessation of all mental
processes. Become aware that the
Self-image and self-concept we have
Of ourselves are only sensations,
Feelings, emotions, images, thoughts
And memories. Below all of this is our

Self-identifying-power; the Absolute
Identity of our Absolute Self.
All that we are, for good or bad, is
The result of what we have thought;
Without thought, there is no world.
There is no good world or bad world,
Only good thoughts or bad thoughts,
The choice is ours!

THE ABSOLUTE IS EVERYWHERE

The Absolute is everywhere
At the sametime; therefore,
It cannot be anywhere at anytime.
Nevertheless, Infinite space
And eternal time can only be
Perceived in the present moment.
Solitude is where the soul
Reflects its infinite magnitude.
Silence is where the eternal
Speaks bout immortality.
Alternately, existence only emerges
In consciousness when intentionally
It's brought into awareness.

WHAT WE THINK IS

Have you thought about this?
We are living in an illusory world
fabricated by our thoughts.

What we think reality is,
is only what we think it is.
What we think it is, that's what it is.

What we perceive doesn't have an
identity until by thought conceived.

Freedom of the mind, is freedom from
the fallacious illusory fantasies and
believes thought has made.

Without thought there is no
existence as humans know it.

BELIEF MANIFESTS

Love, hope and faith
Are potent spiritual powers
Humans have.
Without thought and belief
Dormant they lay.
By our thought and belief,
All things are possible;
From waves of probability,
By thought and belief,
Particles appear spontaneously
Of reality.
Love, hope and faith
Miracles perform
Manifest by belief.

THE IMMUTABLE REALITY

A mind emptied in meditation,
Doesn't represent emptiness in itself;
It only signifies emptiness of contents...
It reveals an ultimate immutable
Reality which no descriptive term
Describes. The ultimate reality
Has no reality in itself, for that
Would be a thought in itself;
It abides beyond the abode of
The Absolute, the Infinite,
The Eternal." The mind in itself
Is no mind; and there is on, no
Mind either, for that would
Make it an object of thought."
This is the immutable Reality

THE DREAM WE SHARE

The dream I dream I share
With you, now you are my
Dream, and I am yours.
The dream we share is
The dream we dream.

In the dream, we drink the
Oceans as nectar; for fun,
We climb the mountains, ride
The clouds and walk the air,
Protected by the atmosphere.

It's in the dream where
All our dreams come true.
If we lose the dream
We awake, to a nightmare!

Painters Paint With A Rush, A Poet With Words.
As a Poet, I paint thought pictures with words—rhythmic emotionally laden words, to capture the singing of birds.

I read messages in the ceaseless rolling of clouds, to serenade the soul. I see the peeking suns at dawn; wonder at the face of man on the moon as it revolves around the earth and the stars beyond, and express to the world divinity I see in the eyes of a child.

I caress a blade of grass as I do a rose. The birds, the clouds, inspire me, and the kiss of the wind as it passes by on the lips of a flower.

SOLEMN BEAUTY
Angels in harmony praise you!
You are solemnly beautiful
The imagination of master
Painters cannot image.

You conform the creation of earth
Exhale the fragrance of a rose
Dim the radiance of the sun.

Bringing joy wherever you dance
Opening the soul to the
Infinite possibilities of a Creator!

WHO AN I

Who am I?
I am an open dimensionless
Being.
I am what I am
By my thoughts and deeds.
I am
Smaller than a Mustard seed,
Larger than the Grand Canyon!
I travel the void
By the imaginary
benchmarks of
the Absolute
the Infinite, the eternal,
As I sit
And inhale the Roses,
Hear the Birds sing!

THE TREE OF KNOWLEDGE

We know
Love, hope, and faith
Are the most constructive powers,
We have.

We know
Ignorance, greed and hatred
Are the most destructive,
We have.

We know
We are free to choose.
What is your choice?

THE TASTE OF IMMORTALITY

Walking down a shady road in
Paradise, coming upon a tree,
It was the tree of Knowledge
And infinite love, whose
Branches reached eternity.

Sitting below its shade, the
Fruits that fell, with ambrosia
Filled my heart and head;
It seemed like immortality
In my hands, I held.

An overwhelm of Devine
Urge was not to keep myself,
My precious find, share
It with the world instead.

My heart with ambrosia filled
I share with you the world
Knowledge and infinite love,
And a taste of Immortality.

A MOMENT WITHIN

When I take a moment within
A moment to go within myself,
Below the subatomic void;
That point within a point where
Time and space converge,
That is where I know I am,
A Spiritual dimensionless being.
That's where nothing, not even death,
Diminishes the conviction
That I am! That I am!

THOU ARE THAT

The most profound words
Ever spoken are "I am,"
This is the sense of Identity
Merging from the universal life
Principle. The second are,
" Thou are That." They
Express the idea that we are
"That" of which nothing greater
Can be thought of, perceived
Or conceived; the ultimate reality.
This is the hidden meaning, of
"I am That I am."
"That" is Absolute truth!

WITHOUT WORDS SPEAKING

In the peacefulness of silence,
We behold the roses blooming;
They display the colors of the
Rainbow as the rays of the sun
Caresses them. We hear
The music of the spheres to
Which we dance with joy.

The rhythmic sounds of silence,
Speaks more than we comprehend;
The beating harmony of drums
Sends secret messages to the mind.

Those who dare will enter leaving
The confusing world behind;
Roaming the skies eternally
Revealing, without words speaking.

Rapid words sung without meaning
Hides the ambiguous mysteries of
The Universe. An illuminative light,
Lights the light in the tunnel; shining
On the open door at the end.

We feel the impulse to Know
More, to Love more, to Be more.
A gate behind the clouds opens
In the sky, and we freely fly
Beyond the horizon to an
Eternal home; bequeathing
Our bodies to earth, with
The roses to bloom again.

WHERE SOULS CONVERGE

Putting the senses to hibernate,
We can travel leaving the sense
Of self behind, to dimensions
Where space and time converge;
Where we can see without the
Sense of sight; we can hear
Without the vibrations of sounds;
Can touch without moving
A hand, know without raising
A thought; we can love without
The stir of an emotion, and
Find joy mingling with the stars,
Heaven where souls converge.

Section IV

VIRTUAL REALITY

VIRTUAL REALITY

THE MARVELOUS BRAIN AND THE ENIGMATIC CELL

*Better to illuminate
than merely to shine, to deliver to others contemplated truths
than merely to contemplate.*
Thomas Aquinas

The brain does not need any adulation or adoration. However, it deserves respect. The brain is the most magnificent, self-cognizing, self-directing, self-regenerative organ in the entire cosmos. It is significantly small and compact; on the average only weighs three pounds, in comparison to the unimaginable, immeasurable dimensions of the Universe, and yet, the entire content of the universes, with the millions of galaxies and suns and planets arises from it.

The genies controlled Twenty-five percent of our ongoing life processes. The balances are controlled by the many given processes of the brain, some of which are, our determination, positive life outlook, mental attitude and beliefs,

There are Fifty Trillion cells in the human body, of these only One Hundred Billion are in the brain consisting of neurons and glia cells. Up to recently, it was the scientific understanding that these were the only two types of cells in the brain, now however, there are indications others has been discovered. The glia cells are commonly called the gray matter, they are important, because they form the structural tissue support for the entangled network of neurons throughout the brain.

Another marvel is that although there are the overwhelming numbers of neurons, each neuron connects to other neurons by means of Ten Thousand synapses — it is perhaps an incalculable number of connections.

Now for the greater marvel, the brain is also small in comparison to the body, but it is the Hundred Billion cells of the brain that controls the Fifty Trillion cells of the body. Moreover, of the many organs of the body, as important and necessary as their functions are, it is only the brain that can know itself, and monitor its actions and their consequences. It is the brain that manifests consciousness from an all-pervading field of universal consciousness, and becomes self-aware of it; thereby the human organism becomes self-conscious. In addition, because we are conscious and self-conscious, we are the only entities that can convert the basic quanta of energy waves to particles bringing into existence the illusion of a concrete universe.

Our beliefs are important; mental attitudes as well as our beliefs are a conditioning and a programming of the brain and it is this that controls our lives not our genies. This is now very much recognized and accepted in scientific circles. However, it is hard for the average person to accept, because it has been so long ingrained, that it is our genies that determine who we are, how we live our lives; and our illnesses and maladies. This knowledge is being brought to a great majority by the renowned cell biologist Dr. Bruce Lipton, a pioneer in stem cell research, and a major influence in the development of Epi-genealogy; who says in his book THE BIOLOGY OF BELIES, "No! Humans are not "stuck" with an innate viciously competitive nature any more than we are stuck with genies that make us sick or make violent."

At this time, without going into the complex mystifying structure of the cell, it is important to know, that everything we do, the inhalation of air, the consumption of bio-chemicals through the nutritional processes is to nourish the cells, and if they become imbalanced or deficient, it manifests as mental and bodily disease. The cells are the basic unit of life; nevertheless, it is the brain that converts it   to its magnificent and beautiful varied forms.

However, we must be alerted, there is an epidemic of mental decline, not only of memory, but of other functions as well. This is going on in the elderly and the middle aged, which can be prevented; by supplying the brain with the proper nutrients, it needs, in the right molecular structure to be able to cross the blood, brain barrier to enter the brain. Furthermore, there is relief by the active use and exercise of mind taking advantage of the brains' Plasticity, which is the brains' capacity to regenerate it's cells. This in turn increases the number of useful synapsis. We must bear in mind that the entire Fifty Trillion cells in the body do regenerative themselves, and have the same nutritional requirements.

At one time, it was thought; we were born with a certain number of brain cells, and if they die in old age, or from lack of use, or abuse, as for instance from drug or alcohol abuse, they were lost forever. Now we know they can regenerate themselves, it is estimated that every Ten years we are a new person cell wise; however, we do not lose our identity because at the core of our being, there is a central processing system that maintains our individual identity.

This gives a scientific flavor to what I have been saying all along; that we can change our lives if we change our thoughts, that we can enjoy peace and contentment if we stop being hateful, we can be loving if we give love.

THE MAGNIFICENT HUMAN

The day we lifted up and walked
Upright on two legs and lifted
Our hands up to the skies,
Reflecting on ourselves,
That day human dignity
Begun. We walked various ways,
Dispersing over the globe.
We conquered the elements,
Climbed the trees, dwelled in caves,
And lit fires, partnered
With buffalos to use as
Clothing their hides. We knew
Instinctively there were more
Mysteries to be uncovered.
Learned that to survive we needed
To respect thing around us,
To do with what we had, and to
Make the best of resources.
Then we landed on the moon!

REFLECTIONS OF OUR REFLECTION

(We are privilege to be participators in the process of life,
Perhaps forever!)

The whole Universe is a mirror!
It only reflects back,
What we imagine we see.

Seeing ourselves in a mirror,
We must ask,
Are we in the mirror, or in the mind?
The same we ask of the world.

Deluded, we take our reflections
For reality, our shadow for mountains,
Thoughts the foundation of the world!

Deception is the mirror of dishonesty.
So are some illusions of our beliefs,
A reflection within a reflection!

Behind the reflections of our reflection
Lies the core of our being, which is
The holographic matrix of existence!

The knowing, the knower and the known are one,
So the perception, the perceiver and the perceived;
As the moon is an offspring of the earth, so
The light from the moon a reflection from the sun!

Thought modifies the thinker, as a reflection
In a mirror modifies the observer, and the
Observer modifies the Universe and the World.

There is unity in the diversity of Humanity,
And that unity is reflected as one world view,
At the bases of which there are an indivisible,
Invisible pulsing moving principle,
An aware self-perpetuating conscious life.
Evolving! Devine!

LIVING IN VIRTUAL REALITY

The goggles of superficiality we ware,
Projects the virtual reality we are in.
Loss of intellectual control
Leads to chaos and turmoil.

The minimal span of awareness displayed
Is focused on the digital games we play.
The friends we'd make live in cyberspace,
And to speak to them, we text
Instead of using a world.

We had lost the sense to write, count,
Divide and sum in kindergarten
We are given electronic tables to do
The work we should have done.

All is just as well, for now we need
Not to carry pocket money,
We live in a money less economy.

The sense of security of a siver dollar
Is lost in multiple zeros and ones!
Many haven't a concept of a Gold coin!

MAKER OF OUR DESTINY

The dilemma,
We are caught between the tidal waves
Of Determinism and Free Will.

Determinism tells us what we have
To do not how to do it. Free will
Tells us we have alternatives to choose,
But once we've chosen the outcome
Is determined. So the answer to this
Dilemma could be, "to be, or not to be."
Just let God have fun, throwing the dice?
Einstein, said, God does not throw dice!

Or perhaps, alternatively, beyond the
Uncertainty, we are alone, neither by
Neither determinism nor free will
Determined, But by our thoughts only
 The makers of our destiny!

Determinism and free will are only,
As the light of day, dark of night,
Dualistic concepts of the mind.

AD-INFINITUM

I love to Philosophize
It's food and music to my soul;
It allows me to dance extensively
Ostensive steps on a cloud.

And Psychology allows me
To introspectively observe
Retrospectively the steps on the floor.

Science, however, on the contrary,
With axiomatic principles, stops
My regress ad-infinitum to a child.

The Answer To The Question, Why Are We Here?

The answer is in realizing that we are the measure of all things. We are the inventors of geometry and mathematics, and we geometries and mathematize the Universe. The Universe per se, in and of itself, as such, has no meaning, purpose or value intrinsically or extrinsically, implicitly or explicitly, other than we attribute to it, and impute it to have. Therefore, we are as two faces of the same coin; we are essential to the Universe as the Universe is to us.

Through our thoughts, and creative imagination, we create ideas and concepts to represent, and try to understand the sensations our senses tell us about the things, occurrences and events outside and within us. These may be factual or untrue, and from many originate our myths and superstitions.

There is always an epistemological shadow clouding our comprehension—an uncertainty about what existence is. Is reality real, or only what we imagine it to be—what we perceive and wish it to be? This is the epistemological Sixty Four Dollar question; we have not with certainty answered yet. All our assumptions are just that, assumptions, leaving us with an existential anxiety. In addition, we grasp at straws trying to find the meaning and purpose of our existence—trying to make sense of our world.

The magnificence of the Humanity
Tthe grandeur of the Universe, apples of the same tree.

VALUE AND THE UNIVERSE

The Universe has no value and is valuing free; it is humans that evaluate and value things, because of our necessity to be supplemented by several complementary systems to survive. The Universe has only physical laws, no ethical or moral laws; its humans which must devise these for their survival.

Epistemologically, ethics and morals answer the question, "How ought we to live," they don't answer the question of, "Why we live." Theology tries to answer this question, but unfortunately, it has never answered straightforwardly, because it deviates from an empirical rational view of the world. It tries to calm our insecurity with platitudes, unverifiable assumptions, and out-of-this-world-fantasies. As each of us comes into conscious life, we are confronted with unfathomable mysteries, but the answer to these is not in the presumptions and questionable assumptions, we make.

We can answer most of our questions about value in the Universe if we view life this way: Life is life, and its strongest impulse is survival. The Universe whatever it is, it is to itself—whatever it is to us, is what we assume it to be; and needed to contribute to our survival. As the world is viewed, so it is. Trying to understand the Universe and we without the experience of our spirituality or reason is like a fish swimming in a vast ocean. The fish will never know what water is, or where he is going—however ironic, it may seem; the fish doesn't know, but de do; we need water to survive. This is where value, and moral and ethical needs kick in. Morality and ethical conduct, and the creation of values are human needs; they serve no Sup-natural purpose. We create and hold valuable the things we perceive necessary for our survival; sometimes we may act contrary to them; however, that is still a matter of choice; there is no determinism here.

However, because we have become so engrossed in the material world, and the perceived materiality of the Universe, which are not permanent, they are transient and forever changing, we forget that the universe at its core is energy. At the core, also every human is energy. We know that energy manifests in various forms. That form, that formative force that transforms energy to conscious life is our spirituality; that which manifests as conscious life, we know intuitively is precious— it is invaluable. Nevertheless, the value of life, the world and the universe depend on it.

THE EAGLES EYE

The eyes of positivism can see
Prestidigitator's sleight of hand,
Deceiving magic mirrors
Distorting bodies of truth.

Rationalization is an assumed
Allusion without valorization;
It validities our expectations
Without empirical, rational proof.

Confirmation evades the eagles' eye.

It's by the formative force of thoughts
Reality is conformed, and by experience,
Except when we are in disguise
Refuting the datum of the senses.

Rationalization applied to the heavens
Brings no closure to earth,
Nor on earth positive truth,
Except for the floating clouds
And warmth of a radiant sun.

WHAT THE BUTTERFLY SAID

Where do we think we are heading,
Without a map or right direction?
Oh! To have the focus of an
Eagle's judicious, certain eye!

The greatest freedom is freedom
Of the mind, by the mind.
The greatest love is unconditional
Freely given on earth or in Heaven
The soul reposes where Angels play.
Silence is the most profound
It conveys to the infinite what
Words loudly fails to say!

THE DOMAIN OF HIGHER INTELLIGENCE

So many times, it has been said,
Existence is a dilemma that leaves
The intellect in an enigma,
Which philosophically has been
Formulated as an emptiness where
There is no foothold to support us.

It has been said; it is not this;
It is not that. It has been more
Succinctly stated by great minds
Of the pass, paraphrased as:
Existence does not exist.
Existence does not, not exists.
Existence does not both exists and
Not exists. Nor does existence
Neither exists, nor not exists.

The enigma deepens as we ask, who
Is the Perceiver? As the perceiver only
Comes into existence in the act of

Perceiving. And the perceiver, the
perceiving and the perceived are
Intractable, indistinguishable one.
No one has said, life is easy;
Nor, how to live, as we should!

In the clearest light of a sun lit day
And the radiance of a noon lit night
Neither Science, nor Philosophy,
Nor Theology, has shown a way
To avoid the anxiety of uncertainty.
That's the domain of higher intelligence!
And, intuitively, inescapably, know
Our existence as we experientially
Know it, is a fabrication of the mind.
Only a reflective power of sparkling neurons
Randomly firing in the night! And,
Ironically, of which, we are of all
The inexorable, responsible cause!

THE SOURCE BEYOND

Gravity is the force holding
The universe together;
Consciousness is greater
It turns energy to matter.
It's the interface between
The spiritual and the physical.
The Absolute is the womb
Which births the soul.

The Infinite and the Eternal
Are benchmarks for the soul
To roam the void. It's bound
To round the earth and must
Return to the seed, the source
Beyond the Absolute,
Where it sprang from.

SPEAK TO THE BIRDS

Everything is in me,
And I am in everything.
When I speak to the clouds,
They wink a knowing eye at me.

When I swim in the river
The river swims with me.
When I climb a mountain,
The mountain climbs with me.

When I speak to the birds,
The flowers and the trees,
Because they are one with me,
They sing back to me songs
I understand.

From me they learn
As I learn from them
To dance on the glow of earth
To fly bodiless thru the sky.

THERE IS NO PLACE

There is no place to hide
From the consequence
Of our deeds.
No one escapes
From his or her self,
That is,
From our self-concept;
What we think we are,
Unless the soul is, free
From the mind!

THE MULTIPLYING CELL

To know and to do are to Be,
There is no knowing without being,
No being without knowing.
Movement and change are
The weaving strands of reality.
Every cell in our body knows
What to do to multiply infinitely
Eternity fulfilling our longing
For immortality.

TIME AND WORD

Time
Is brief
As contour of clouds.
Or, long
traverses agglomeration of Galaxies
Lasts more than a sparkle of light.
It can be young or old
Innocent as the child
Wise
As an eagle in its nest.

Waits for no one
It illuminates the truth
At length erases it.

 Gives the day languorous hours
In the night rapidly evaporates.
It gives periods of Glory
To the history
Between spans of interval
To the oblivion, dethrone her.

Time oblige us to see
More that we know because
In the void of space it
Makes an eternal home
It does not separate.

But
With time and a word
Humanity can be saved!

It is for which the poet
takes time through the time
With sincerity of truthful word
And rhythm of honorability
More than adornments of charity
penetrates the roots of the soul
For the salvation of Humanity

THE TERMS OF MY LIFE

Having been so long shut up within
The constraints of my body,
Bound, as it were, by the chains
Of my mind, I cannot see the light
 Of the sun; nor can I roam the skies
 Freely as the birds. I fancy so often
An escape by the images of my
Imagination; but all the assumptions,
The skies, the oceans and the horizons
Are only an Illusory projection,
A mirage of my desires. If I extract
Myself from my perceptions, and
Choose the angle of my views, I can sit
And enjoy all the fantasies passing
By, I can see the birds will forever
Roam the skies, and feel the warm
Light of the sun, and know I can,
Endure the terms of my life!

O, TO REGAIN FREEDOM OF THE MIND

Why do we believe
In a previous and after life?
At birth, our mind was born
Innocent, pure and free;
we need not proof to see.

Consequently, by proclamations,
Dogmas and creeds contaminated.
With the parental, ethnic and
The social milk, we were feed.
Our freedom of choice was set
To replicate myth and superstition.

A condition which bounds
The mind for life with whims
Of our ancestry. O, to regain
The freedom of the mind!

LIGHTS FLASHING

In my world, every raindrop
is a sparking diamond
Falling from the sky kissing
The face of the earth
Merrily laughter is heard.

Frogs crook a hymn as
Hummingbirds caress a flower.
But the greatest surprise of all
Are rainbow flashing lights
In the Heavens
Telling us all is well.

THE ONE IN ALL

If you cannot find the me in you,
And I can't find the you in me,
We might be looking for shadows
Instead of the real thing. Nether
The me within me nor the you within
You exists superficially.

If you'll look much deeper beyond
The illusions in the mirror,
You'll find the me in you
And the you in me; all other
Superficialities are unsubstantiated;
As an illusive passing wind.
For, the One in all, and the all in one
Is at the core of one reality!

IF I COULD HEAR THE WHISPER OF THE STARS

If I could hear the whisper of the stars
When they make love to one another
Promiscuous as this may seem
It's not different than love at the bottom of the sea.

The stretch of the Giraffe kissing in the sky,
The caressing of Elephant's trunks entwined.
Humming birds confiding their choice of mate to the
winds,
And the sunflower winking at the sun attention getting.
Here the drive to survive is not a moral issue.

And the pursuit of heaven is a daily affaire, love
everywhere:
Everywhere on earth, the sea, and in the stratosphere.

I wish I were a humming bird kissing every flower
A Dauphin buoying in and out the seas, swimming in
pair,
Or I just as well might be, a cloud, the rain, or sun
Rising for the world to see with open arms, I care!

ABIDING BEYOND THE ETERNAL

There is "That" which the self
Calls the "Self", which is no-self,
And there is no, no-self either;
For that would be an object of thought

That which is called the Self is
An open dimensionless Being,
Arising from a void in itself void.
The Thatness is only an encumbrance in the Void!

To go beyond the void of the void,
And get to a destination of no-dimension,
Stop all thinking, and realize you are,
Only a transcending awareness,
A self-realizing awareness.

Thoughts, shapes and forms are projections of the mind,
Only thoughts floating, as reflections in an ocean;
Beyond time and pace, where the Self is not!
There you can abide beyond the infinite,
And the eternal will be your home!

Life only transforms from one state to another
Like space it does not diminish or extinguish;
In itself invisible, has no shape or form,
Yet projects through its immortal eye
The beauty of hanging clouds, the rays of the sun!

DO YOU NEED A MIRROR?

You don't need a mirror
To know who you are, if
You do, you are in deep trouble;
You cannot even be lost in sleep.

For there your are in the dream,
You may fool others to think
You are other than you are,
But you cannot fool yourself.

Only you know when you are
Honest with yourself;
Only you can tell if you are
Having a genuine relationship

With yourself and the world.
Are an authentic human,
Or are you just a flake
Of deceptive dirt.

Genuineness is not hard,
Wishing others, happiness makes us happy,
Having compassion for others

WHAT THE BUTTERFLY SAID

Make us compassionate.
Loving unconditionally
Make us honest and genuine.

THE "SELF" NEVER AGES

When we look in the mirror of life
What we see is a reflexion of
What we assume ourselves to be.

We do not see our real selves,
Which is deeply hidden below
Nuisances of shape, form and color.

What we see in the mirror is
What we think we are; some say,
O, I am ugly; O, I am beautiful.

Some say, I am old, and impaired,
Have quite a few wrinkles and more
They don't realize the body ages,
The Spiritual self never ever does.

It always retain its original purity,
Brilliant as the day conceived,
It never ages to all eternity!

The more thoughts we think,
The more submerge It becomes.
Cease thinking and the Self emerges
Brilliant, pure, forevermore!

Never lost in the anguish of despair.
The mind and the emotions do not
Support the pain, the cries, the laughter,
From birth to death. Self endures. More!

WHAT YOU ARE COUNTS

What you are called,
Or what you call
Yourself does no matter;
It's "what you are" counts.

The formation of stormy
Clouds, the break of ocean
Waves does not shatter,
The infinity of the sky,
Nor the peace at the
Bottom of the ocean.

Like wise, you are not
Changed or destroyed
By what you are called.
What you think determines
Who you are. Nothing disturbs
The perfect you within,
It's allays peaceful and serene.

This Poem carries a deep spiritual meaning, and at the same time a very practical one. The practical one is about "Bulling." If parents read this to their children, it should convey to them a sense of their self-worth, and boost their self-esteems. The message, nothing anyone says or does, or any circumstance or event, can hurt us, unless we allow it, and we react to it.

WHEREAS I AM SUSTAINS

Whereas,
Happiness is the fruit of our labor,
Contentment is a spiritual state,
And joy is their reflection.

Whereas,
It's only in the stillness of quietude
And solitude, we receive the gifts
Of bliss and tranquility.

Whereas,
Other strivings are unnecessary,
Veiling the void awareness
Of our true nature,

Whereas,
By the images of imagination
The "I am" sustains,
Our reflections of a Universe!

A PASSING THOUGHT

"Since all that we are, are the results
Of what we have thought".
We must be careful what we think;
What we think of and say to others,

But more importantly what we think
Of and say to ourselves.
One negative thought can destroy
The intent of a hundred good ones.

I like to explain what we do to ourselves with our thoughts, without being aware of it or of the consequences, by the analogy of driving a car. If you drive a car by pressing the accelerator and alternately pressing the break, you are not going anywhere, and you are destroying the car and can be the cause of an accident. That is what we do to our minds and bodies, and to those around us, by entertaining positive and negative thought at   the same time. You know the saying, "Be careful of what you wish for." I want to emphasize, yes; we are all free to think, however, thoughts are not forever sculptured in tone; and, we must stop imposing our beliefs on others; only then, we will have peace in the World. Please think of this, for it is at the root of all our discomfort, frustrations, animosity, anger, hatred, greed, diseases, and wars. If you think this is important enough to take your time to share it, please do!

THE CELEBRATION OF LIFE

We must celebrate life (Individually and collectively) and give gratitude for all the insignificant things that makes up our life, as well as the beautiful and the great; most of the time we take the insignificant as irritants and annoyances, and the beautiful and the great for granted. We do not realize the grandeur of our life. We are too concerned with trivialities, the banal, and pain and suffering, to appreciate all the pleasures of joy—we cry with pain instead of crying with joy. We should be grateful for every breath of air we have been given the will to inhale, and every grain of sand we tread upon.

We must take the time to reflect on all the people who touch us and the ones we have touched, for in some small or large way every encounter leaves an imprint in our minds and souls!

We are on the same voyage, on a planet that revolves around the sun, and the miracle repeats itself day in and day out. In addition, the greatest gift we have been given is the Power of Love. The problem is some of us do not know we have it, and others do not know how to share it. Many of us, on the other hand, confuse sensuality with love, not knowing that the true power of love is unconditional.

Section V

AN ADDENDUM

We have no chance to rehearse

The character we play

In the drama of life.

Nor by chance, we play!
Thomas P. Lind

ADDENDUM

Don't look at the stars for salvation, you are a supernova in the constellation. Through the essence of an unmodified awareness, you can perceive the undifferentiated absoluteness of your being, arising from the center of the void, filling infinite space and eternal time. Your light can be seen expanding, crossing the universe, filling the minds of every human with conscious energy, their hearts with unconditional love.

I have been writing critically about the sociopolitical and the human condition. I am also concern about why great civilization fall and disintegrate. However, I have made it clear; we should not blame the society or the civilizations, for they are not entities in themselves, but the people that comprise them. Why?

Because we become indolent and indulgent nations of people; governed not by the rule of law, but by deception, pretension, ignorance, greed and hatred. Honesty of purpose and sincerity of intent serves no purpose in our lives; neither does peace and contentment. Because we are driven by an unquenchable pursuit for instant gratification through objects of pleasure.

We make of life a parody and of truth a mockery; and of Law, unlawful administrative ambiguous rules, administered by buffoons at their whim. However, do not blame them; blame the smart ones who adjudicate for themselves prerogative powers for their ends. This is why societies and civilizations crumble.

This section five may not be written as eruditely as Gibbons' The History of the Decline and Fall of the Roman Empire. However, it is written to impress in us deeply some of the social issues that are plaguing our societies, causing dissention, discontent, frustration and anger. My only satisfaction would be, if you see the irony, and realize they need not be so, they can be changed. I write for us to realize, we are magnificent beautiful spiritual human being, and can live, and should life, maximizing our unlimited human potential.

THE BATTLE FOR FREEDOM OF THE MIND

This is in tribute to all who has battled for the cause of freedom. We have to admit; misguided Religious Beliefs has destroyed more souls than it has saved. Ethnic, Racial and Religious Bigotry, which originates from Ignorance, Greed and Hatred, are a curse we have to overcome. The greatest freedom will come when the minds and souls of men are free. The ultimate freedom is freedom of the Mind from the Mind!

God is not narrow minded, or else he wouldn't have made us as diverse as we are, and given us Free Will. To guide our lives the best we see fit, He does not dictate to us, for that would contradict the Free Will He gave us. That means we have the freedom to express ourselves religiously according to our beliefs. No one in a reasonable state of mind would believe its Gods will; have to have to kill the people he has crated, because they do not believe what some of us believe; and, ironically, reward us for it. This belief comes from an arrogant confused state of mind.

Religious Freedom and Freedom from Religion are two different concepts we have to learn to keep separate in our minds and in our hearts. Those who hate and massacre people because of Religious Intolerance must believe in a God of Hate, not the God of Love the majority believes in. Freedom of Religion in any part of the world does not mean the imposition by religion; it means freedom from Religion. Moreover, freedom from Religion means to choose the religion of our choice, and be free to believe in God as the spirit of God moves us in our minds and hearts; not what some faction dictates; nor Political pressure, and scientific mumbo-jumbo oppress our Spirituality. We must regain the freedom of our spirituality and the mind.

IT'S CIVILIZATION

We ate raw meat before
The discovery of fire;
Fruits under the trees
Doing us well. We stood
Under waterfalls before we
Invented the showerhead. What
Did we do for soap so long?
Only God knows,

We smelled the female scent
She the pheromones before
We discovered deodorant.
The women tanned hides
For garments all to wear,
Help on the hunt before the
Advent of clippers, nail polish
For their toes and fingers.

Children ran, chasing each
Other around, climbing trees;
Swam! Crossing the rivers for fun.
Now they sit getting supposedly
An education and, their animation

From videogames and television;
For fun cell texting daylong.
This, for all the aliens daring to
Come, must know, is civilization.
Have we lost, in the transition?

HOOKED AT TEM

I stare at fate and staring back at me
I see her bloody eyes,
Dirty hands,
Her prison cells, the back ally narcotics,

Hooking into my flesh like falcon claws,
Redemption fell,
With the broken school fences,
And there at ten I'm hooked on drug,
Reciting the Ten Commandments!

Delinquency was only part of what was sold,
Bought never a subtle or outright question took,
Answered! Required! Requested!

Going along with the pushers and the pullers,
Victimized by that passion which knows no end.

Innocence is an expensive gift
None can afford to lose.
Raving dogs or just to any god,
Or faith with bloody Eyes.

Tears are such infective weapons
Against
The garbage we are force to live.
Flinching dignity!

Cringing, recoiling back, fate fences in.
With hung heads and shame,
Who will take the blame?

Who are the brave who would fight tooth and claws,
The establishment tearing complacency to shreds?

How can I regain,
What fate fences in?

How can you give me back,
That life you hooked on drugs?
Yourself addicted!

BROKEN LIMBS

Rampant as the winds and the rolling hills,
Surging waves break the back of the mighty
Oceans.
Calm might the rivers reflections be, but
Turbulent
The roar of volcanoes banishing their beds.

Climbing clouds, dark, spreading to hide the sky,
Veils the sun's blushing face, anger red.

It's a day to remember for a storm is brewing
Kettles of discontent, leaving no consolation.
Bird's nests falling with
Broken limbs from mighty but gracious tree,
Troubled by the agony around them.

Beneath the rumble of a broken home little
Birds crying endure. Custody doesn't help
A hungry heart—hard to understand.
But the lament is heard, loud from those banished
From the trembling land where once was planted
Green fields of corn.

When the winds have had
Its fun, and leave with a frown, calmly the misplaced
Returns:
Somewhat broke-hearted glad to be back
Home—but the love blown by the wind is not found—
Never returns.
Somewhere, out there, there is a baby bird, and a child,
Hoping to be rescued!

Hoping to restore what the storm has stolen
From them…!

THE MINDS OF STEEL OR JELLO

A mind of steel makes going up the stair worthwhile,
effortlessly,
It depends on what we expect to find.
And coming down, a slide down the banister just for fun,
           (It is the hard thump of the butt hitting
the ground, falling down
The steps, which hurts the most.)
Can the embarrassment be saved?

Minds of steel makes toy weapon
Withstanding the winds carrying souls aloof,
Like hand gliders out of control; Bombs!
Dropping them down at Gibraltar, sometimes not that far,
Just dropping bombs on the nearest village by the ocean.

These minds of steel are little things, but harder than
stone,   Sometimes wiggly as jello, shattering as
Easy as glass.

There are so many things this mind of steel can do,
Many varied and wearied things, large and small, not a
blade of Grass and the beetles to munch them down,

It invents lawnmowers.

Making Universes takes much longer; sometimes it creates
A Big Bang explosion to play it safe. Without
Explosives!
Harder to figure how to make invisible matter visible!
Viable!

How to make from nothing, huller hoops, lollypops and
roller-blades for children to play.
Sometimes it sees what cannot be seen,
Like, those funny rings around Jupiter, which serves no
purpose But it's fun to do.

Making suns takes a few more tricks, and quite a lot of
bricks,
The sum has to be, hot to burn the debris,
Or,
Grow everything it touches. Leaving nutrients on the
skin.

The mind steel makes the steal, to make guns with which
to kill, Makes humvees flame throwers, and military
personnel vehicles to Play war-games.
It makes the carriers, the warships, and the submarines
Carrying the nuclear weapons.

And then there is other thing it makes, such as,
Chemistry sets and stethoscopes, to play doctors and
nurses,
Scientists to be.

It makes labels saying, do not try this at home, leaves it
to the Professionals.
Keep it away from children playing; it is hazardous to
their health.
They will suffocate if put it over their heads. The mind of
steel, Although it controls the world, is ephemeral, no
where to be found;
Perhaps it is just plain jello.

Sensitive to, it will
Self-destruct in any minute, if not handled care.

WARNING: Keep the brain away, damages done to it,
will be Considered an
Act of God, and are not reimbursable. Not covered by
insurance.

These are some of the things the minds of steel can make;
Don't explode with Satanic, sadistic laughter.
.Whoops! Sorry!
A Freudian slip,
The line should be: Satiric, sarcastic laughter.
Perhaps it should be. The Mind That Steals!

YOU ARE CALLED A WAR VET

Have you ever been lost in a runaway train,
Going faster than the speed of light?
Suddenly it stops.

It lets you off in a wheelchair in the middle of a dilemma,
You don't know where you were going, or where you
were coming form.
You don't remember the street and number either. The
day you was born? You ask someone standing by for
directions, he doesn't know either, he is a stranger,
Just arrived. At least he is not in a wheelchair.

You look around the strange city blocks desolate as if
everyone
Were hiding. Some lonely person daring to venture
saying Hi!
You ask: Do you know where I am? And he answers,
what's your name?

As from a fog by rout a spark spouts out, Rank and
Number. I am sergeant
John Doe, First Battalion. You can't remember the
number, but it's on
The Dog Tag around your neck. You wish it wasn't
called a dog tag.

You say to yourself under your breath, "I deserve better
than that."

He says almost whispering, "You are a War Vet struck
by shrapnel in the head.
You served your country proudly, but your country
doesn't proudly
Serve you. It lets you down, in a runways train, in the
middle
Of nowhere."
He says, "You are a War Hero!"
But you hate the word,
Somehow it stirs within you sorrow for the lives
destroyed to earn the name.

It has destroyed you too; you lost arms and legs, wife and
kids, your identity
You try to hold on to your dignity—
But no one knows who you are!
The war's over, who cares!

They call you a "War Vet"; you lost your name,
Some call you a "War Hero"; for whose gain?

NO JUSTICE TO BE FOUND

Rationalization is a form of self-justification
but nowhere is justice to be found.
The Lion devouring an innocent Impala
Is a selfish act of self-justification
But where is the justice for the Impala?

We rage with anger and aggression
Because we are driven by hunger to survive
But where is the justice for the hunger?
Why it's necessary to destroy to survive?
That leaves us begging the question.

Is it inhumane to be inhuman
To those who are inhumane to us?
Where is the justice for our existence;
Justice for the innumerable refugees,
Who must scamper the earth to survive?

IT USE TO BE WE PRAYED

It use to be many eons far away
We were prey for the predators,
Until we learned the predators
Could be our prey. It was so
Long ago we scarce remember,
But what we know we are predators
Still. We still stalk and hide and
Torment and kill.

It use to be many eons far away
All we were afraid of was natures
Wrath, her volcanoes, hurricanes,
Earthquakes and tornados. Torrential
Rains flooding and tidal waves.
Now we are afraid of weapons
Of masse destruction. Atom,
Hydrogen and fitly dirty bombs,
And of virulent infestations and
Infiltrations by terrorist's holy men.

It use to be many eons far away
We fought for land, monarchies,
And kingdoms jeweled crowns,

We fought in and out of churches,
Temples, mosques and synagogues;
And we prayed to our gods to give
 Us dominance over our fellowmen.

Nothing has changed that much,
We still have an Iraq war, a war
In Afghanistan. North Korea and
Iran scrambling to get their hands on
The Atom Bomb, along with India
And Pakistan. And al Queda and
The Tailban jihadist terrorizing
The world, along isis holymen.
 And the stocks on wall
Street rises and falls every day,
Memories of wispiness,
Along with a declining Democracy!
What else is new!

THOMAS P. LIND

A STREAK IN THE HUMAN SPIRIT

In the mine of the human spirit
There're many streaks, one as good as gold,
Leading to our dreams fulfillment.
That perhaps may be the redeeming streak of all.
Also there're streaks of silver lining the rim of heaven,
And other metals that serve us well, when mixed
With our hopes and aspirations, a sprinkle of love.

But there is another strong one, which has no name,
Some call it evil, some call it sin.
It's that mean streak of desperation
Driving us to destroy ourselves.

It dulls the sharpness of the intellect
Confounds the logic of common sense.

It has led us to divert the current of rivers,
Defile the face of mountains,
Killing defenseless species just for fun

To build towers of babble to find what we can't fine,
Building confusing highways leading nowhere,

WHAT THE BUTTERFLY SAID

This is the streak leading us to our destruction.

A streak we hope our progeny will overcome,
But what can we leave them, if we've destroyed the
world!

IF HOPE EVADES

There is none so treacherous as when
Our reason betrays us.
There is none so confused as when
Our mind fails us.
There is no heart so broken as when
Love evades us.

I am also cheated as when
I can't find words to express my feelings.

But I am not beguiled by mysteries when
It matter not one way or another
If they are ever solved.
It would matter to us if we solved
The mysteries of the Universe,
Only if it made us more loving.

But none would have lost more then he
Who has never found hope?
Or have loved a speck of earth.

INEXPLICABLE

My incomprehensible sensing self eking
Ebullient multicolor feelings sweet as honey,
Or as heavy serum of circulating blood keeping
Tempest of anger from over boiling. I stake
My life duelling on life's highways with strangers
I don't know.

It is still early and the day is slow,
But the traffic going always in every direction,
Accumulates quickly denser than the morning fog,
All the comfort of oblivious sleeping dissipates
In the constant grind of shifting gears and stopping
Peddles. Smelling scent of squalling tires burning.

The asphalt streets already exhuming heat hotter than
The sun and the angered raged drivers wheeling
In and out squeezing crossing eight lanes of cars,
Trying to recover lost time for exits missed.

This is how my day begins and ends. Duelling!
Make a living stuck in traffic jam. But I always
Wonder why we travel to work, why can't we work
Where we are coming from? Avoid getting mad,
And burning tires in traffic jam? Inexplicable!

THOMAS P. LIND

THE EVENING NEWS

(This is satire of the News Media and of Society itself.
As you know by now, I am a Social critic, and I reserve
not my tongue, when it comes to Dishonesty and
Pretention.)

For those who want to know,
There is always news broadcasting on the evening show.
The newscasters taking turn parading their thoughts
About all the latest crime and fads: Some who died today
Are mentioned, because of fame. They never ever
Mention the homeless.

The frivolous and the pretentious make it humorous,
The farcical and the obvious, ridiculously ironic!

Like the car towed away for over parking in a none
parking zone,
(Who cares.) And a broken water main!
And the guy taking his unpaid parking tickets to light his
fifteenth cigarette.
The gangster lighting his cigar with a hundred dollar bill.

The Seven Eleven store keeper shooting someone dead
for stealing
 A six-pack. A gracious woman fell off her seven-inch
high heel shoes dead. Her insurance refused to pay.

 Today, high jackers, high jacked a Mercedes Benz,
abandoning it on the Brooklyn Bridge.
There was a shooting on Fifth Avenue and Thirteenth
Street by a   by a   to be blind.
Someone was stealing his pencil selling money. He said
to the reporter:
"I don't like crooks!" Remember Nixon! Teenagers with
a baseball bat killed a homeless man for fun.
They said: "He should have been in a home, we don't
like vandals"

A righteous man leaving a church raped and killed a
prostitute reposting her body in a sanctuary
Blessing him in   the pool of holy water. He said, "I don't
like sinful people." Two men vandalized the same church
and stole the donation box. They said, the church had
more money than they had. And they can put it to better
use; they need it to buy a barrel of crack. "There are
many kind hearted people
Who will replace the money, buying "indulgencies",
they said.

The people in Colorado are in a perpetual recreational
altered state of consciousness, or are they just plain
stoned from smoking pot; on the other hand, the big drug
companies are raving mad, because the FDA couldn't

give them a patent, or an exclusive license, to get rich
form medical marijuana.

We hate to end this broadcast with bad news: Today
terrorist destroyed the World
Trade Center in New York City, and car bombs exploded
in the middle of London and Madrid.

And according to the latest census, there are over Seven
Billion misplaced persons all over the globe, all-suffering
from lost identity, or is it identity theft. They are refuges
from themselves. The good news, is
A good many are waiting for Saint Peter to open the
gates of heaven to let them in, others, are just waiting
around for the next shuttle to Mars! They are devotees of
the religion of Science.

"That's about all the news for now" The newscasters
said.
 "We'll see you tomorrow right here, same tine, Have a
good night!" Because we are the guardians of Free
Speech, we have the right to influence your mind and
life;
We have told you, from our omniscient perspective, Only
what we want you to know!

SEXUAL ORIENTATIONS

Truth stares us in the face and we don't know it,
Because we are arrogant.

When we sleep in a strange bed, we can't explain why,
Because we deny it.

Somethings taken for discomforts haunt us for life,
Should we ignore them? Not knowing they are virtues.
These are the things going on in our heads
In the dark. Alone!

Answers there are none!

We pretend it's a dream we can't remember,
Like the entire crazy things, we think we know,
Which we don't recall that well.

Whatever we say is but a lie.
Like a secret we discover about a friend
Who is not a friend any longer,
Because we denied him.

He is trying to determine his sexual orientation.

We think about this watching a woman walking a dog
While we stroll the park. The dog barks.
We pat the dog on the head, trying to make friends,
While she stares away aloft in wonder.

She pulls the dog away squealing, just about the time

When it would have said: Hello! We are left stranded.

We watch the dog going.
She has pretty legs.

What secret might she be hiding
Under that skirt? Perhaps she is bisexual,
A transvestite or a mother to be?

We wonder who coined the word
Sexual preference?

It's so confusing.
She didn't stand long enough to make friends,
For us to know.
Truth stares us in the face and we don't know it,
Because we are arrogant.

Those who would be pregnant control it,
The child they long for is adopted.
Dogs really are man's best friends,
They know the truth, keeping secrets well.

This truth however we can explain:
Sex, politics and religion don't blend that well!
However, now it is political correct
To ask. What's your sexual orientation?

FUMBLING IN JUNGLES OF COLOR

Life is like the works of a great artist,
Their paintings are designed to trick us
Into believing we see something,
Which really isn't there.

Their painted clouds and rays of the sun
Are like hope, they dazzle us
With a depth of dimensions
Without a beginning or an end:

For all we know, we don't' know!

What do we really see?
Like the eternal gaze
Of the near blind—we are
Fumbling in jungles of color!

THE ETERNAL NOW

Only in the present moment,
We live, embrace it with joy.

Be not sorrowful for your yesterdays,
Nor distracted by tomorrows concerns;

For you live only in your thoughts,
The ones occupying your attention.
An instant, in the eternal now!
Let your thoughts be of unconditional love.

It's only when we live in love,
And compassion we live infinitely,
In the eternal now!

After all said, it seems we are missing something, we need something. Perhaps, it is what I have said many times before, a balanced mind and an open heart, and what a popular song says, "What the world needs now is love, sweet love." Here is an insight, which was revealed to me—if we empathize with every grain of sand; and we send love and compassion to every human and living thing on earth; the Universe will compensate us with love and abundance; and even the gods will reveal their secrets to us.

So here you have it, the secret of how to live in love and abundance in the eternal now.

Love is to humans as gravity is to the Universe. Scientists do not know what gravity is, nor psychologists know what love is, but without them, it would be chaos. The Universe would be formless and disordered without the power of gravity; and so would be humans without the power of love. To conclude, love is no ordinary thing, it is mysterious and mystical, and when we love unconditionally, we share and partake in the Devine! Knowing this should give us the courage to live peacefully, regardless of the circumstance.

Ye are gods for the asking. Be elite, a chosen, privileged inspired and protected one. Open your minds and hearts and be in atonement with the creative forces of the Universe. Let the creative force flow through you to elevate your humanity to its unlimited potential. Accept the grandeur of the Universe, and the magnificence our humanity as one. Humans are the only witnesses, the knowers, the movers and the makers of the valleys and mountains, the rivers and oceans, the billions of stars and galaxies we conceive and perceive.

NEITHER BEGINNING NOR END

To the brightest minds

The beginning and ending

Of the Universe are unknown;

Neither of life, we know

The beginning nor the end.

Of life, we know only what

Are given to know, therefore,

It would be incumbent

To respect what we know,

And honor what we don't.

Perhaps we should flow,

As the clouds and the birds,

Flow into the ocean

As the rivers forever do.

BY REGRESSION EXPLAINED

Power and magic are the tools we use
To school the young, control the very old
At the start, the middle, the very end.

We imprison all their hopes and their dreams,
In the longest fairytales ever told;
How a magic spell was caste creating
In an instant smaller than Nano time
All the galaxies, planets and the stars.

Of how we began from nothing or space
And have a loud explosion-taking place.

No one know the beginning or the end
Of why do the simplest grain of sand
Form the earth we stand upon.

The single life cell can multiply,
To trillion cells a human to form;
Only by regression it's explained!

MOTIVATION THAT DRIVE ME MAD

I have tried to be creative writing
Concepts, words and sentences freely,
Rthymitacally flowing out my head.

Compose sense-captivating poetry,
Beautiful literature to be read.
Hoping the thoughts matter more for sure,
Not the flowery words I had said.

If in a heart sentiments I've stirred,
Making you think, laugh and cry, not sad,
Then my rewards would rightly be served.

I would have conveyed my sentiments
From a starving heart to another,
That to me is important as life—
The motivation that drives me mad!

NONETHELESS MYSTIFIED

Walking wondering all these many years
Why I am mystified roaming the earth
By the majesty of the waterfall,
Tall slender, an unknown creator.

I contrast this with the volcano's roar,
Hot seam raising form the caldrons floor.
Nonetheless, made by the same creator.

Waterfalls mist sprinkling flowers to grow,
Volcanoes spewing stone the earth to stow.
Never satisfied of the answers given,
Nonetheless, I roam the world, mystified.

THOMAS P. LIND

TWO LINE POEMS

SNAPSHOTS IN WORDS OF ARROGANCE, GREED,
HATRED,
THE IGNORANT AND THE DOWNRIGHT
DECEITFUL.

SECRETS

Squinting eyes can see more,
They can tell where the middle-tones are.

DECEPTION

Myth is pretension,
Superstition deception.

LOGIC

Some religious beliefs sifted through reason
Logically doesn't make sense.

ASSUMPTION

Presumptuously assuming the unverifiable,
We have committed an effrontery to truth.

FAITH

Faith is belief in the supernatural
Controlling our destiny without reason.

EXISTENCE

Nothing in existence makes any sense,
Nor any of the assumptions we've made.

LIES

It is a lie angles are rushing
Where human foolishly dare to tread.

VICES

The seven sins: Lust, Gluttony, Greed, Slot, Wrath,
Envy, Pride.
Deception is ignored plus several millions more.

GUIDANCE

Even birds need guidance,
They don't fly randomly.

REALISM

If realism is seeing with the eyes open,
What do we see with the eyes closed?

.

IGNORANCE

The physically blind don't walk with sure steps,
The mentally, don't even see the sun.

GREED

Who says the belly craves food,
Ignores the eyes.

HATRED

We do not like whatever,
We are predisposed to hate.

ANGER

Anger can't be hidden for long,
It pops out unexpectedly.

ARROGANCE

Dancing naked arrogantly in the park,
Missing the green grass stepping on broken glass!

DECLINATION

The destruction of Civilizations
Not by war, by indolence and indulgence.

HERO-WORSHIPPING

Venerating the prowess of others
Living vicariously following the herd.

WORSHIPPING

We worship the gods of imagination.
Pray at the altar of our beliefs.

BUILDERS

We build Kingdoms in a spiritual world,
Hoping to go to when we are dead.

IRONY

In life we live in Hell
It's a waste of time going to Heaven dead.

CRIES

We've cried Wolf so often
The gods now ignore the howl.

UNIVERSES

Mental constructs, architectural
Buildings in imaginary space.

FUNDAMENTAL

Both the past and the future are arrangements
In the present, by fragments of memory.

CONSCIOUSNESS

Consciousness is a mirror reflecting

What the knowing life principle apprehends.

INDULGENCE

The desire for instant gratification
Makes of indolence a virtue.

THE PERENNIAL QUESTION

Asking, "WHO AM I" is the same as, asking who made
the Universe,
What we get is a reverberating echo breaking the silence.
No Heavenly songs!

GENIUS

The tools of a Genius,
Determination, commitment and persistency.

THE SPIRITUAL

What was once called Spiritual
Is now the digital world of cyberspace.

ABOUT THE AUTHOR

Thomas P. Lind is A Social Critic, he writes in Poetic form;
he was Director of Dietary Services at The New York United
Hospital Medical Center of Port Chester, N. Y., where he also
taught classes in Biofeedback theory and practice at the school of
Encephalography. He has degrees in Psychology. He was
a member of the International College of Applied
Nutrition and of the American Hospital Association, and
an associate member of the Academy of Orthomolecular
Psychiatry. He was a member of the American Association
of Sex Educators, Counselors and Therapists of
Washington, D.C., and is a Certified Sex Therapist. He
holds a certificate in Rational-Emotive Counseling from
The Institute for Advanced Study in Rational
Psychotherapy, chartered by the Regents of the University
of the State of New York.
Other works: GREEN IS THE GARDEN, a volume of
Poems; THE FACTS OF LIFE YOU ARE BEING
DENIED, non-fiction, a philosophical/psychological
approach to life. AN EPIC OF THE MIND. IF THE
HEAVENS BREAK OPEN. BEGGING THE
QUESTION. FLYING WITH SEAGULLS. ROOTS OF
ETERNITY. WHAT THE BUTTERFLY SAID.

www.ingramcontent.com/pod-product-compliance
Lightning Source LLC
Chambersburg PA
CBHW020038040426
42331CB00030B/17